Weird Wonders of the Deep

An Imagination Library Series

Coelacanth: The Living Fossil

by Valerie J. Weber

GARETH**STEVENS**

PUBLISHING

A WRC Media Company

Please visit our web site at: www.garethstevens.com
For a free color catalog describing Gareth Stevens Publishing's
list of high-quality books and multimedia programs,
call 1-800-542-2595 (USA) or 1-800-387-3178 (Canada).
Gareth Stevens Publishing's fax: (414) 332-3567.

Library of Congress Cataloging-in-Publication Data

Weber, Valerie.
    Coelacanth: the living fossil / by Valerie J. Weber.
        p. cm. — (Weird wonders of the deep: an imagination library series)
    Includes bibliographical references and index.
    ISBN 0-8368-4561-7 (lib. bdg.)
    1. Coelacanth—Juvenile literature. I. Title.
QL638.L26W43   2005
597.3'9—dc22   2004060678

First published in 2005 by
Gareth Stevens Publishing
A WRC Media Company
330 West Olive Street, Suite 100
Milwaukee, WI 53212 USA

Cover design and page layout: Scott M. Krall
Series editors: JoAnn Early Macken and Mark J. Sachner
Picture Researcher: Diane Laska-Swanke

Photo credits: Cover, pp. 5, 7, 9, 11, 13, 19, 21 © Mark V. Erdmann/SeaPics.com;
p. 15 © Doug Perrine/SeaPics.com; p. 17 © Patrice Ceisel/Visuals Unlimited

Printed in the United States of America
16.50
1 2 3 4 5 6 7 8 9 09 08 07 06 05

Front cover: Fishermen in Indonesia call the coelacanth
the "king of the sea." Until very recently, they did
not realize this type of fish was millions of years old.

Table of Contents

Words that appear in the glossary are printed in **boldface** type the first time they occur in the text.

A Living Fossil

In 1938, fishermen brought a strange fish up from the deep sea near South Africa in the Indian Ocean. A museum worker in South Africa took one look at their catch and thought the animal was something scientists had never before seen alive. A fish scientist agreed. This was a living fossil, a coelacanth (SEE-luh-kanth).

Everyone thought coelacanths were long gone. After all, they swam the seas before the dinosaurs lived. **Fossils** formed from their bodies show that they lived 400 million years ago. Scientists thought they had died out about 65 million years ago along with the dinosaurs.

4

In 1938, a fishing captain found a coelacanth like this one flopping on the deck of his ship. His deep sea fishing nets had trapped it. He did not suspect how unusual his catch would prove to be.

An Odd Find

Pale blue scales with white spots covered the coelacanth's 5-foot (1.5-meter) body like heavy armor. The fish shone with silver and blue-green sparkles. It weighed 127 pounds (57 kilograms).

A strange **joint** lay between the coelacanth's head and its body. No other living animal was built like this. The joint let the coelacanth lift its upper jaw and drop its bottom jaw at the same time. This action widened the coelacanth's mouth so it could grab and swallow large **prey**. Tiny sharp teeth filled the wide mouth.

The museum worker thought its tail looked like a puppy dog's tail. The coelacanth could wag it back and forth like one, too!

The coelacanth's rear fin looks like a fan of feathers around a tiny tail. Its scales are very large and hard.

Fins Like Limbs?

What made the coelacanth even more interesting were its fins. They seemed more like an animal's legs or people's arms and legs than fins on other fish. The fins stuck out from the body like stalks.

Scientists later found that the fins also moved the way people walk. As the left front fin moves forward, so does the right rear fin. The coelacanth can also turn its fins in a half circle. Very few fish swim like this.

At first, scientists thought coelacanths walked along the ocean floor with these motions. Now they know these fish hover above the seabed. A coelacanth can even swim on its back!

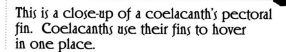

This is a close-up of a coelacanth's pectoral fin. Coelacanths use their fins to hover in one place.

Spineless

Unlike other fish — and people — the coelacanth does not have a backbone. Instead, a hollow tube runs down the back of its body. Oil fills the tube.

Little light shines down into the deep sea where coelacanths live. Their large, shiny blue eyes gather in as much light as possible. They shine in the dark like a cat's eyes do. Their eyes help them find their prey. A coelacanth can also use a special **organ** on its snout to hunt. The organ senses the weak electricity that its prey's bodies give off.

The coelacanth's eyes look like blue crystal balls. An organ in front of its eyes helps it find its prey.

Baby Coelacanths

Coelacanths differ from most other fish by giving birth to live young instead of eggs.

About twenty-six baby coelacanths can live in eggs in their mother's body. Slightly bigger than tennis balls, these eggs are unusually large.

Like chicken eggs, coelacanth eggs contain yolks. The yolks provide food to the baby coelacanth growing inside the egg. When the baby coelacanth is big enough, about 1 foot (30 centimeters) long, the mother pushes it from her body. Because coelacanth babies can swim right after birth, they can escape many **predators**. This helps the coelacanths **survive**.

Female coelacanths grow larger than male coelacanths. They probably need more room for their large eggs.

Protected in Deep Water

How has this kind of fish existed for so long without being discovered? Coelacanths need little food to survive, which is good because little lives in the depths. Animals that do not need to eat much tend to live longer.

During the day, coelacanths live in deep caves about 660 feet (200 meters) below the water's surface. At night, they swim deeper, almost 2,000 feet (610 m) down, to hunt. They feed on squids, swell sharks, cuttlefish, lantern fish, and other fish. Few predators hunt the coelacanth.

Coelacanths' bodies cannot stand the warmer water on the surface of the ocean. They never swim where people can see them and rarely where fishermen can catch them.

Coelacanths hunt swell sharks like this one for food.

The Missing Link?

The discovery of the coelacanth in 1938 created a huge stir. Newspaper writers and scientists called the coelacanth "the missing link."

Scientists had long wondered how sea animals **evolved** into animals with **lungs** that could walk on land. Coelacanths move much differently than most other fish and have been on Earth a long time. Because of this, some scientists thought they might be a link between sea creatures and early land animals. Early land animals might have evolved from coelacanths.

Now, most scientists believe a different group called **lungfishes** are more closely related to land animals than coelacanths are.

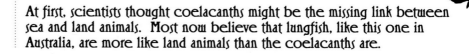

At first, scientists thought coelacanths might be the missing link between sea and land animals. Most now believe that lungfish, like this one in Australia, are more like land animals than the coelacanths are.

A Second Discovery

When the first coelacanths were discovered off the South African coast, scientists thought that was the only place they lived. Then in 1997, two fish scientists found one in a fish market in northern Sulawesi, Indonesia. Indonesia lies on the other side of the Indian Ocean.

The Indonesian fish was a different color. Gold flecks speckled its brown body. Everything else looked the same.

Millions of years ago, changes in the land covering Earth had separated the two groups. If two groups survived in two such different parts of the sea, could there be more somewhere else?

Coelacanths cannot survive in warm, shallow water. If they are brought to the surface, they usually die.

Finding a Coelacanth

One way people can see a live coelacanth is to go down in a tiny submarine. Those who do so search for the fish along the steep slopes of undersea **volcanoes**. Often, the coelacanths are nowhere to be found. More people have been to outer space than have seen a coelacanth in its deep-sea **habitat**.

Scientists thought coelacanths had died out long ago. Their discovery raises more questions. Do coelacanths live somewhere else besides the waters near Southern Africa and Indonesia? Are there other fossil fish living deep in the seas? What else might we find living in the ocean? The mysteries of the deep ocean still wait for us.

This coelacanth swims with one of the scientists who discovered it near Indonesia in 1997. Scientists are hoping to discover coelacanths in other waters.

More to Read and View

Books (Nonfiction) *Deep Sea Adventures: A Chapter Book.* *True Tale Series* (series). Kristen Hall (Scholastic Library Publishing)
Fossil Fish Found Alive: Discovering the Coelacanth. Sally M. Walker (Carolrhoda Books)

Videos (Nonfiction) *Fish Out of Time: A Quest for the Coelacanth.* Jerome F. Hamilin

Places to Write and Visit

Here are three places to contact for more information:

American Museum of Natural History
Central Park West
at 79th Street
New York, NY 10024
1-212-765-5100
www.amnh.org

Field Museum of Natural History
1400 South Lake Shore Drive
Chicago, IL 60605-2496
1-312-922-9410
www.fieldmuseum.org

Steinhart Aquarium California Academy of Sciences
875 Howard Street
San Francisco, CA
94103-3009
1-414-221-5100
www.calacademy.org/ aquarium

Web Sites

Web sites change frequently, but we believe the following web sites are going to last. You can also use good search engines, such as **Yahooligans! [www.yahooligans.com]** or **Google [www.google.com]**, to find more information about coelacanths. Here are some keywords to help you: *coelacanth, lungfish,* and *living fossils.*

www.amonline.net.au/fishes/fishfacts/fish/ coela.htm

The Australian Museum's fish site tells the story of the discovery of the coelacanths in two different places.

www.dinofish.com

This Web site of the Coelacanth Rescue Mission includes a report from a coelacanth fan going down in a submarine. Click on the virtual web camera to see how coelacanths swim.

www.nature.ca/notebooks/english/ coela.htm

This Canadian Museum of Nature site includes a picture of the coelacanth and a map of where it lives.

www.pbs.org/wgbh/nova/fish

Click on various links in this *Nova* television program web site and find out why coelacanths are different from other fish, take a coelacanth quiz, and read the letters between the woman who discovered the coelacanth and the fish scientist who confirmed her discovery.

Glossary

You can find these words on the pages listed. Reading a word in a sentence helps you understand it even better.

evolved (eeh-VAHLVD) — changed over a very long period of time to become better able to survive 16

fossils (FOS-uhls) — traces of animals or plants stuck in and preserved in Earth's crust 4, 20

habitat (HAB-uh-tat) — the place where an animal or plant lives 20

joint (JOYNT) — the part where two or more bones come together. Your knees and elbows are joints. 6

lungfishes (LUHNG-fishes) — fish of the Amazon, western and central Africa, and Australia that have body parts that can breathe air as well as gills 16

lungs (LUNGS) — two sacs in the chest that help animals, including people, breathe. Lungs fill with air. 16

organ — a body part that performs a special function. 10

predators (PRED-uh-turz) — animals that hunt other animals for food 12, 14

prey (PRAY) — animals that are hunted by other animals for food 6, 10

survive (suhr-VIVE) — continued to exist 12, 14, 18

volcanoes (vohl-KAE-nose) openings in the earth's surface where melted rock, gases, and ashes are forced out 20

Index